Microsoft Dynamics AX 2012 Lean

A complete review of the essential setups
needed to implement AX 2012 Lean

Andrew F. Weber

Table of Contents

Introduction

This is an AX 2012 lean module essentials handbook. All basic and requisite setups, with typical transaction examples, are included. The document assumes knowledge of the following:

Item and bom setup

Master planning

Financial setups and dimensions

No advanced warehousing setups are used in the examples. Discrete planning and Sub-contracting setups are not covered in this document.

Setup explanations and field input recommendations precede each screen copy. Data inputs and nomenclature can be found on the screen copies. If a field is not mentioned, it is not needed for that setup example. The table of contents is also a setup sequence summary.

About the Author: Mr. Weber is an AX and D365 developer and implementer. He can be reached at AndrewFWeber@gmail.com

Product version: Microsoft Dynamics AX 2012 R3

Production Parameters, Lean

Note: Instructions precede screen copies

1.   Go to Production control > Setup > Production control parameters.

2.   Click the Lean manufacturing tab.

3.   Input

      1.   Production instruction default

            1.   'File' or 'Note' is typically used

            2.   If supplemental document print outs are required with Kanbans, print management updates will be required (print management is not covered in this document)

      2.   Quantity unit of measure default

            1.   Note: if used, 'ea' may need a unit measure update

      3.   Time unit of measure default

4.   Click Close.

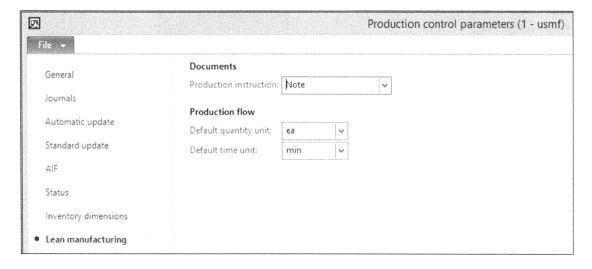

Production Flow Models

Note: Instructions precede screen copies

1. Go to Production control > Setup > Lean manufacturing > Production flow models.

2. Click New.

3. In the Production flow model field, type a value.

4. In the Model type field, select an option.

5. In the Capacity shortage reaction field, select an option.

6. In the Planning period type field, select an option.

7. In the Planning time fence field, enter a number.

8. Click Close.

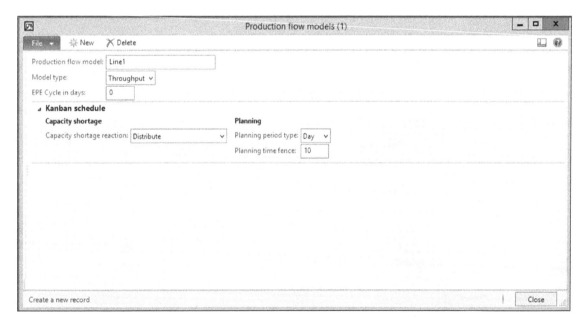

Field descriptions:

EPE

- Is a lead time offset that is applied during scheduling

MODEL TYPE

- 'Throughput' schedules and consumes capacity by quantity
- 'Hours' schedules and consumes capacity by time

PLANNING TIME FENCE

- Is the period during which kanban cards can be automatically planned
  - Kanban Rule for auto planning flag setups are not applied outside this fence. (see Kanban Rules section)

CAPACITY SHORTAGE REACTION

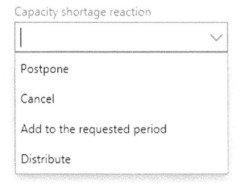

- Finite, Postpone full quantity to first available date
- Finite, Cancel order if capacity is not available
- **In**finite capacity, Add to the requested period
- Finite, Distribute quantity

Work Cells

Note: Instructions precede screen copies

1.   Go to Organization Administration > Common > Resources > Resource groups.

2.   Click New.

3.   In the Resource group field, type a value.

4.   In the Description field, type a value.

5.   In the Site field, enter or select a value.

6.   Select Yes in the Work cell field.

7.   In the Input warehouse field, enter or select a value.

8.   In the Input location field, enter or select a value.

9.   In the Output warehouse field, enter or select a value.

10.   In the Output location field, enter or select a value.

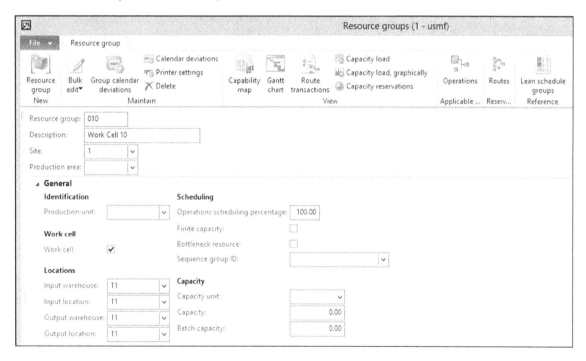

11.   In the Run time category field, enter or select a value.

    1.   Note, cost category financial setups are not covered in this document

    2.   Setup and Quantity cost categories are <u>not</u> used by Lean

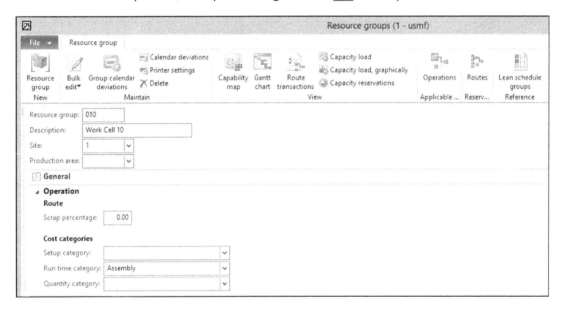

12.   In the Calendar field, enter or select a value.

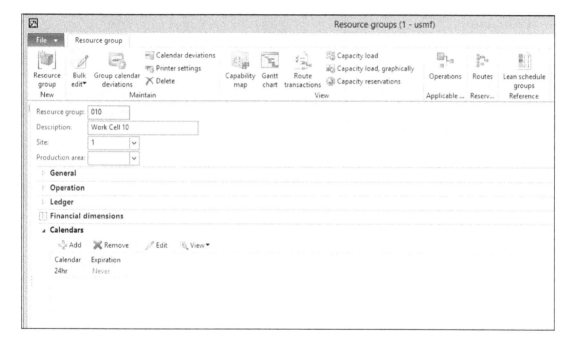

13.   In the Production flow model field, enter or select a value.

14.   In the Capacity period field, select Throughput or Hours.

15.   For Throughput only, in the Average throughput quantity field, enter a number.

16.   In the Unit field, enter or select a value.

17.   Click Close.

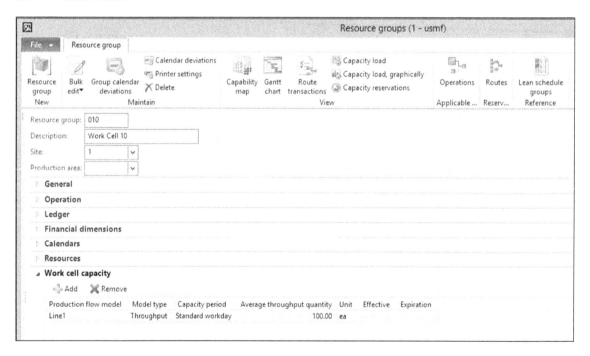

Note, these settings also affect Kanban Schedule Board display parameters.

Value Streams

Note: Instructions precede screen copies

1.   Go to Production control > Setup > Lean Manufacturing > Organization > Value streams.

2.   Click New.

3.   In the Name field, type a value.

4.   Click Close.

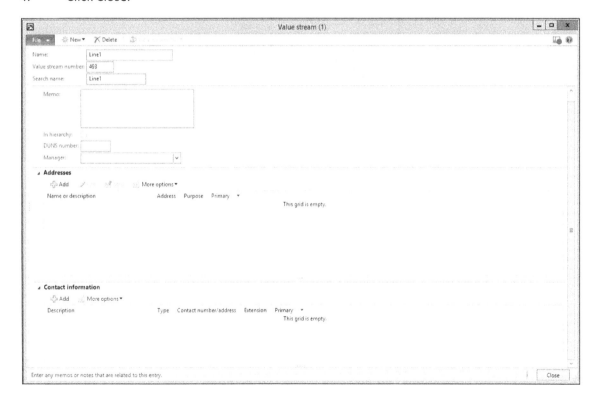

Note: Value streams can be used as a financial dimension.

Production Groups

Note: Instructions precede screen copies

1. Go to Production control > Setup > Production > Production groups.

   1. Is part of financial setup, which is not covered in this document.

   2. Production Groups are used by Production Flows.

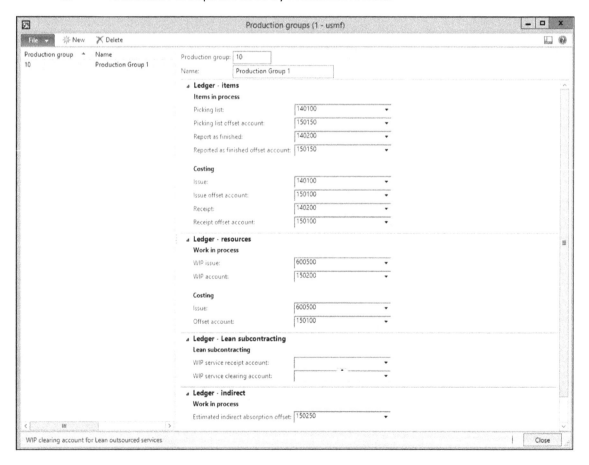

Production Flow Version

Note: Instructions precede screen copies

1.   Go to Production control > Setup > Lean Manufacturing > Production flows.

2.   Click New.

3.   In the Name field, type a value.

4.   In the Description field, type a value.

5.   In the Value stream field, enter or select a value.

6.   In the Production group field, enter or select a value.

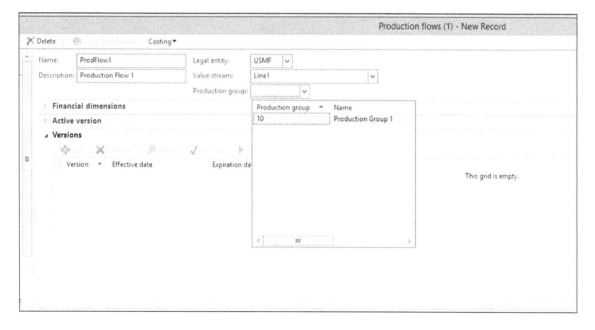

7.   Note: costs and transactions can be accessed from the Costing pull down

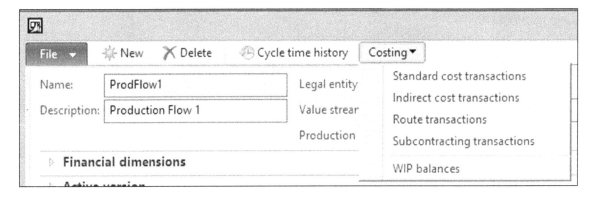

8.   In Versions Click Add.

9.   Click OK.

      1.   Note, on completion of activities add, Production Flow will need to be activated
        on the Version fast tab.

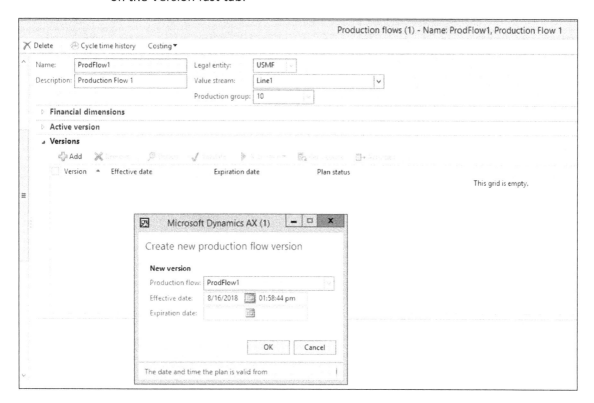

10. Open Version details.

11. In the Takt unit field, enter or select a value. (if applicable)

12. Update times if required

13. Click Save.

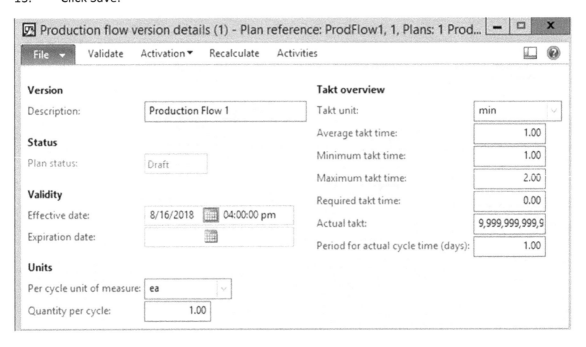

Production flow version details (1) - Plan reference: ProdFlow1, 1, Plans: 1 Prod...

File ▾   Validate   Activation ▾   Recalculate   Activities

Version

Description: Production Flow 1

Status

Plan status: Draft

Validity

Effective date: 8/16/2018   04:00:00 pm

Expiration date:

Units

Per cycle unit of measure: ea

Quantity per cycle: 1.00

Takt overview

Takt unit: min

Average takt time: 1.00

Minimum takt time: 1.00

Maximum takt time: 2.00

Required takt time: 0.00

Actual takt: 9,999,999,999,9

Period for actual cycle time (days):   1.00

14.   Add Financial Dimensions if applicable via the fast tab display option (Financial
      Dimensions setup is not covered in this document)

15.   Click Close.

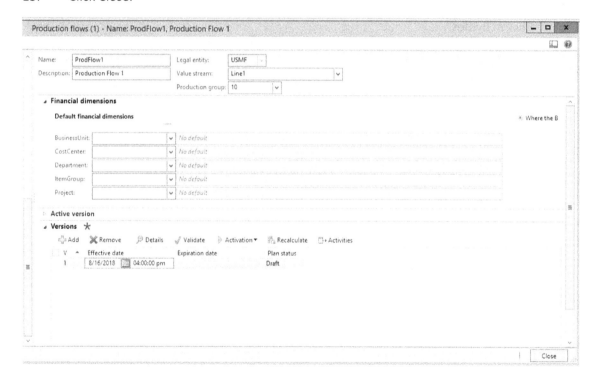

Production Flow Activities - Single

Note: Instructions precede screen copies

1.   Click Activities.

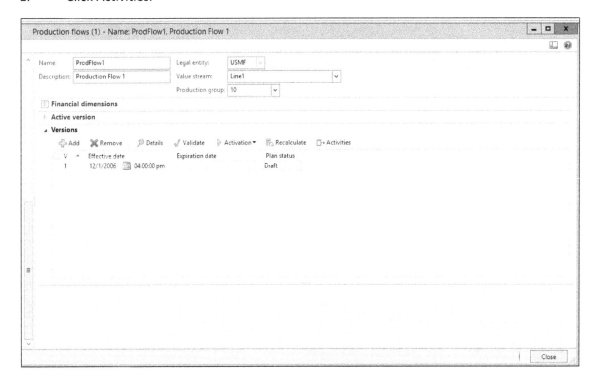

2.   Click Create new plan activity.

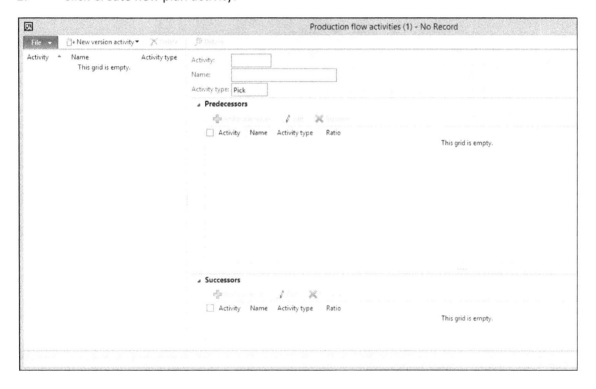

3.   Click Next.

4.	In the Name field, type a value.

5.	Click Next.

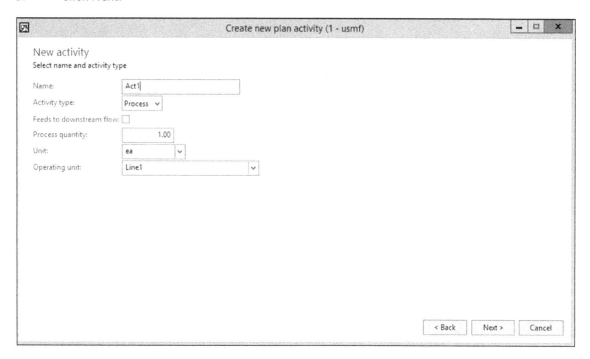

6.   In the Work cell field, enter or select a value.

7.   Click Next.

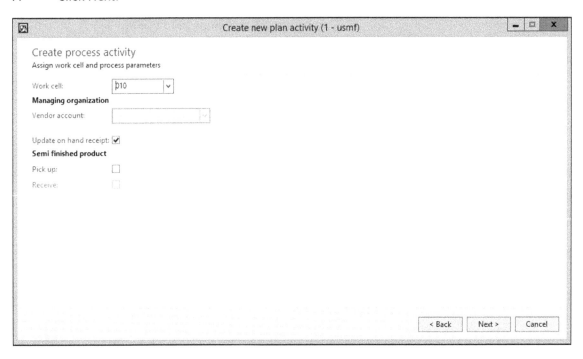

8. Assign item numbers that need to be manually picked. Otherwise no parts need to be entered, and backflush will automatically consume the bill.

9. Click Next.

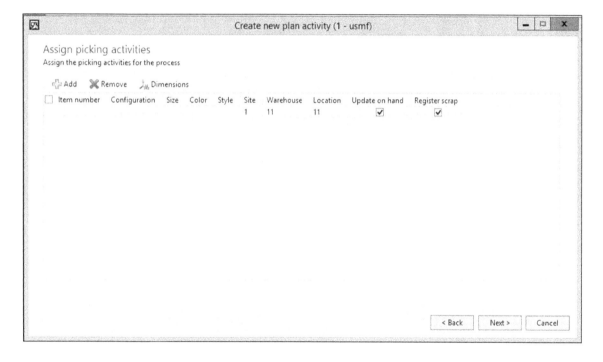

10.   Assign a time to the activity. (i.e. time by work cell)

    1.   Times by part are enabled using Lean Schedule Groups

11.   Click Next.

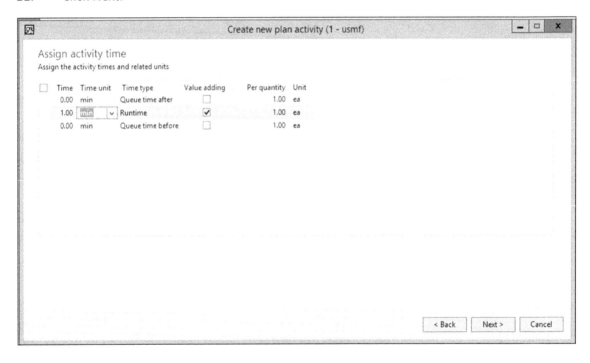

12.   Click Finish.

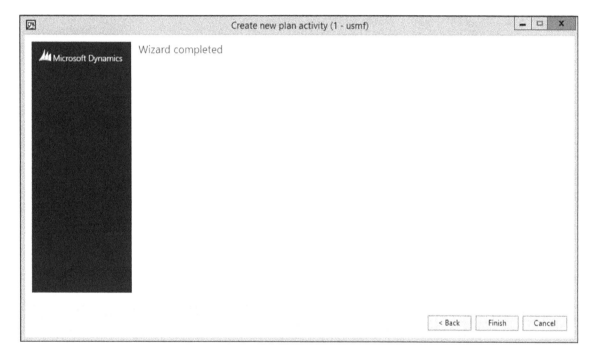

13.   Click Close.

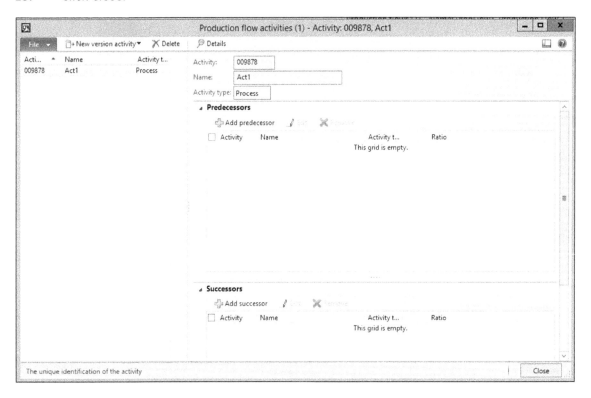

14.　Click Validate. (optional)

15.　Click OK on pop up.

16.　Infolog will indicate success or failure.

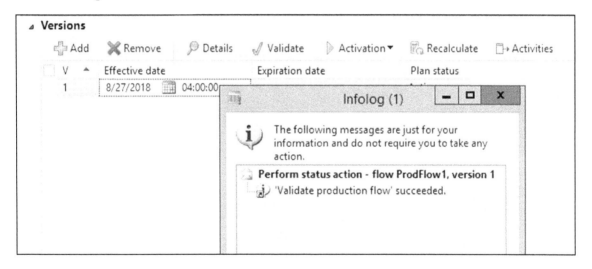

17. Click Activate.

18. Infolog will indicate success or failure.

19. Note plan status = Active on success.

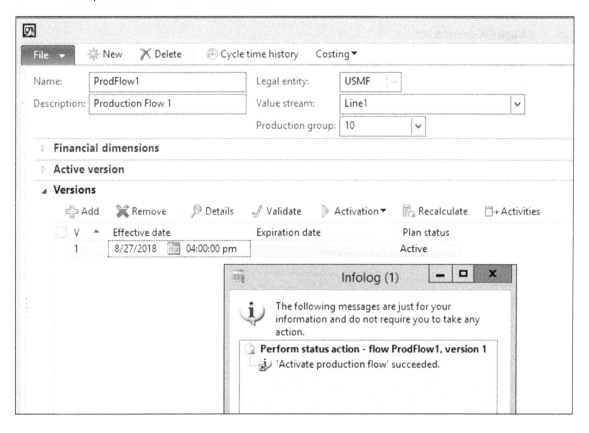

Production Flow Activities - Multi

Note: Instructions precede screen copies

1.   Click Create new plan activity. (activity 1)

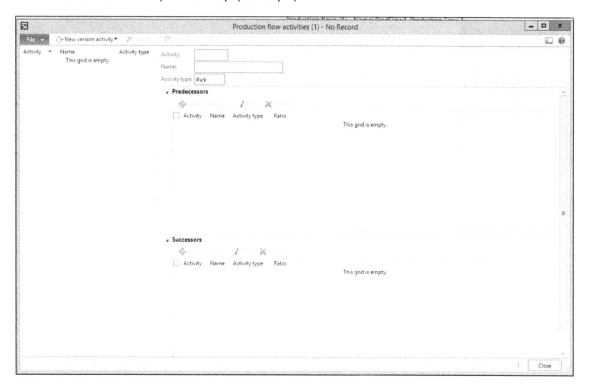

2.   Click Next.

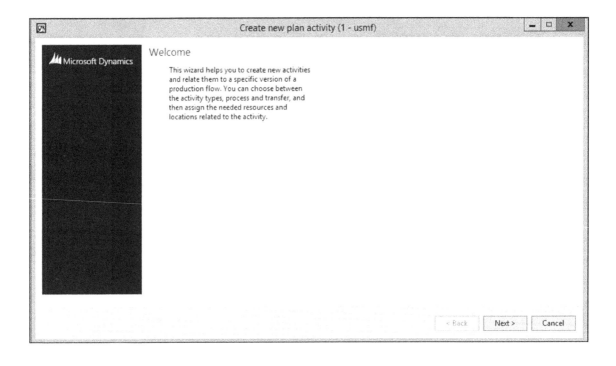

3. In the Name field, type a value.

4. Click Next.

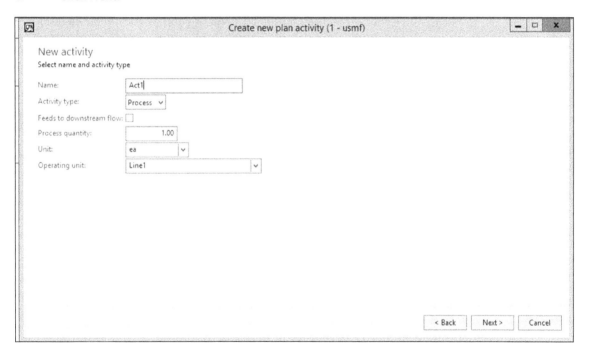

5. In the Work cell field, enter or select a value.

6. Select No in the Update on hand receipt field.

    1. Only the last activity is enabled for Update On Hand

7. Pick-up is unchanged

8. Select Yes in the Receive field.

    1. Product will be sent downstream (i.e. 'received' by the next activity) as semi-finished (i.e. a phantom)

9. Click Next.

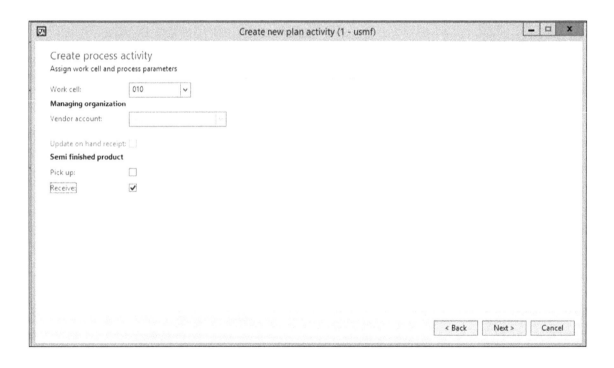

10. Enter parts that need to be picked manually if applicable. If blank the bill is flushed automatically.

11. Click Next.

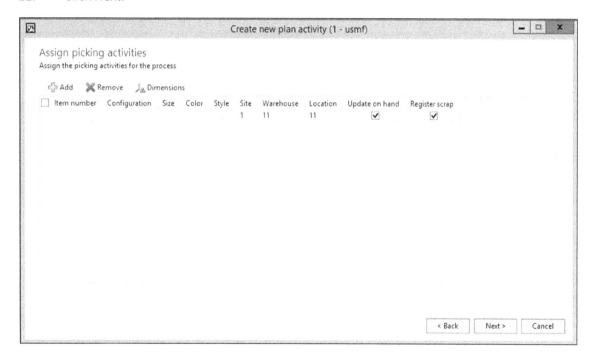

12. Update Time(s). (i.e. time by work cell)

    1. Times by part are enabled using Lean Schedule Groups

13. Click Next.

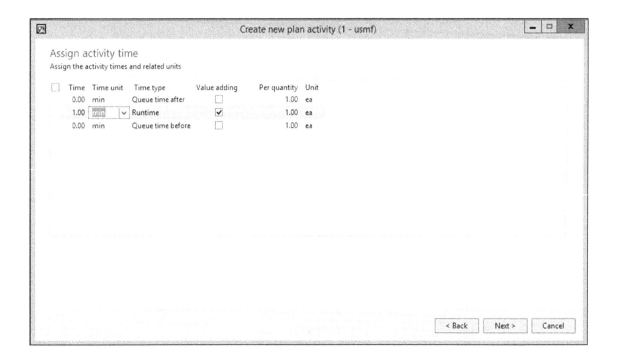

14.   Click Finish.

15.   Click Create new plan activity. (activity 2)

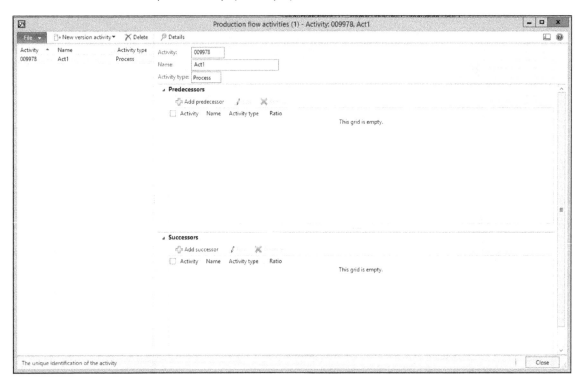

16.   Click Next.

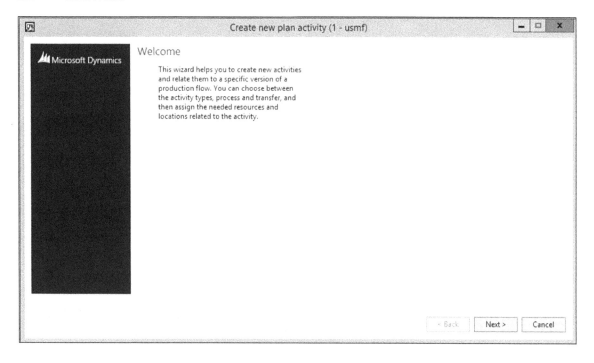

17.   In the Name field, type a value.

18.   Click Next.

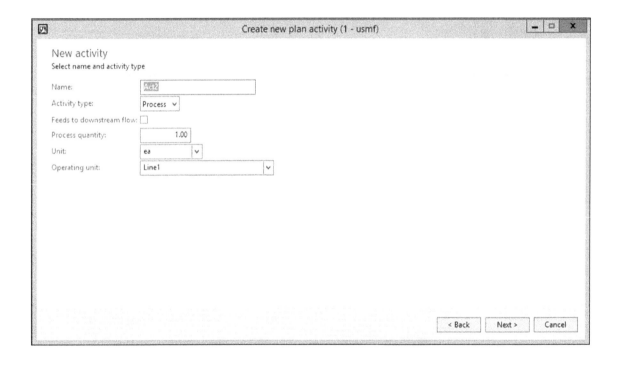

19.   In the Work cell field, enter or select a value.

20.   Select No in the Update on hand receipt field.

21.   Select Yes in the Pick-up field.

     1.   Semi-finished is picked up from upstream activity

22.   Select Yes in the Receive field.

     1.   Semi-finished is sent to next activity downstream

23.   Click Next.

24.   Update Time(s).

25.   Click Next.

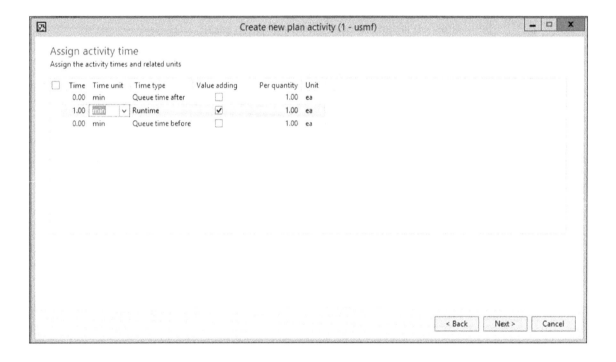

26.   Click Finish.

27.   Click Create new plan activity. (activity 3)

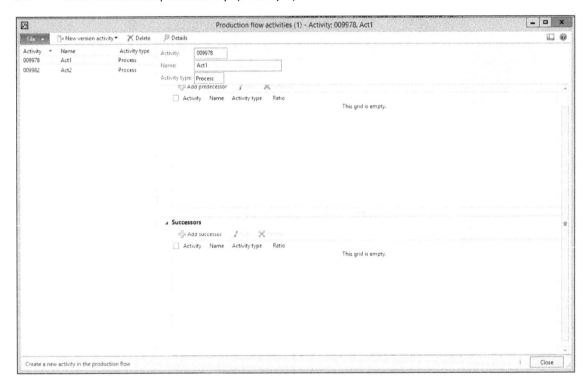

28.   Click Next.

29. In the Name field, type a value.

30. Click Next.

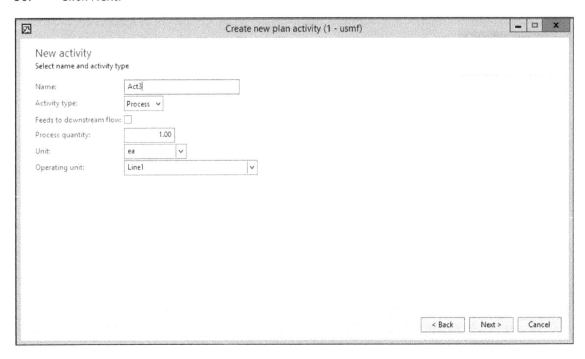

31.   In the Work cell field, enter or select a value.

32.   Update On Hand is unchanged at Yes. Act3 is the last activity.

33.   Select <u>Yes</u> in the <u>Pick-up</u> field.

34.   Receive is unchanged at No – there is nothing to send downstream.

35.   Click Next.

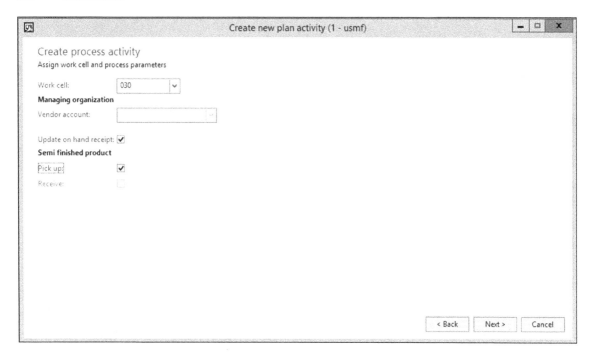

36. Update Time(s).

37. Click Next.

38.   Click Finish.

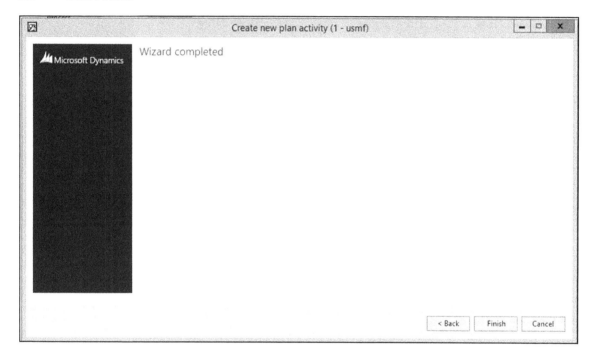

39. Click Add <u>Successor</u> for activity 1

   1. <u>Predecessor</u> will be applied automatically for Act2 when setup is completed.

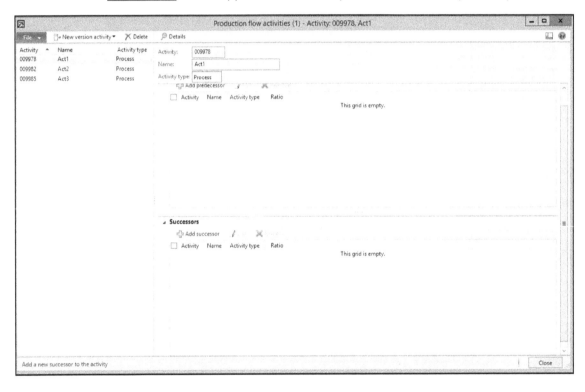

40.   In the Activity field, enter or select a value. (Act2)

41.   In the Cycle time ratio field, enter a number. (if applicable)

     1.   Cycle is number of upstream cycles needed to feed the downstream activity.

42.   Click OK.

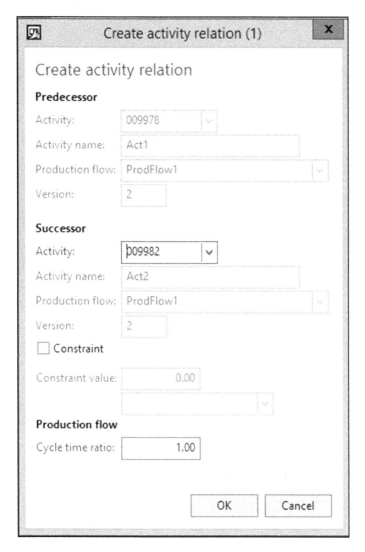

43.   Select the second activity. (note activity 1 is listed as a predecessor)

44.   Click Add successor.

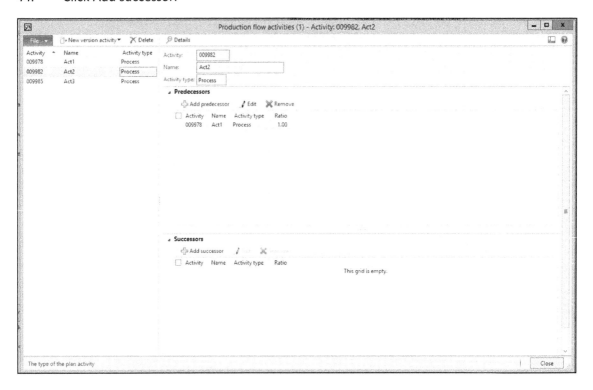

45. In the Activity field, enter or select a value. (Act3)

46. In the Cycle time ratio field, enter a number. (if applicable)

47. Click OK.

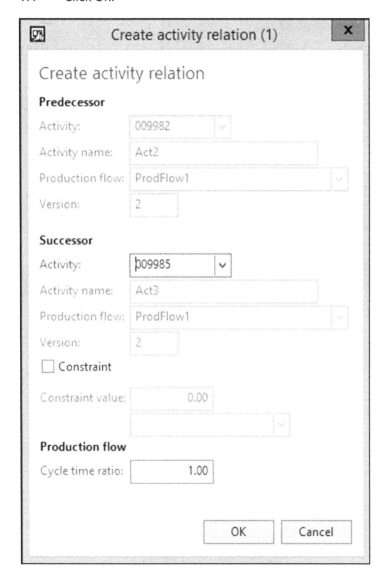

48.   Note that Act2 now has both a predecessor and successor.

49.   Activity 3 will list Act2 as its predecessor.

50.   Click Close.

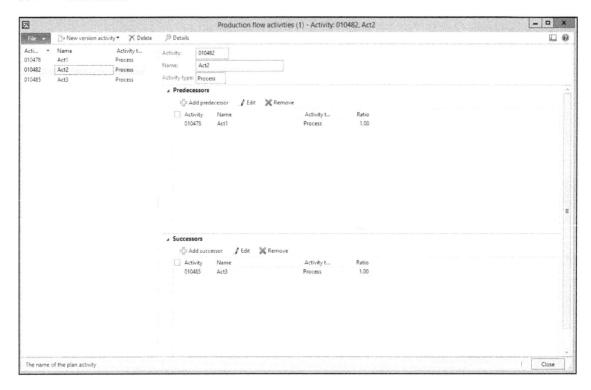

51.   Note that both production flows require activation.

Production Flow Activities - Transfer

Note: Instructions precede screen copies

Single activity example. Production flows with process activities can also be ended with transfer activities. Defined as a Withdrawal kanban on kanban rules.

1.   Click Create new plan activity.

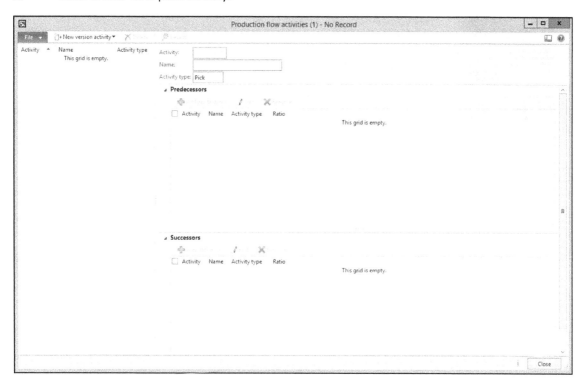

2.   Click Next.

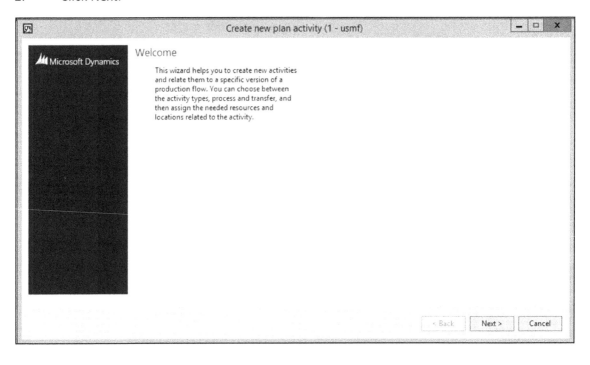

3. In the Name field, type a value.

4. In the Activity type field, select Transfer.

5. Click Next.

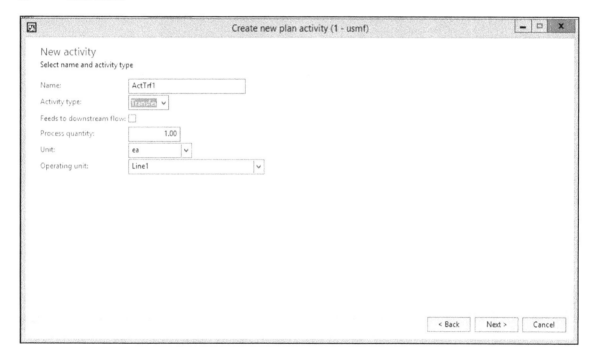

6.   Click Next.

1.   Use Work Cells if work cell defaults are needed. Otherwise can be skipped.

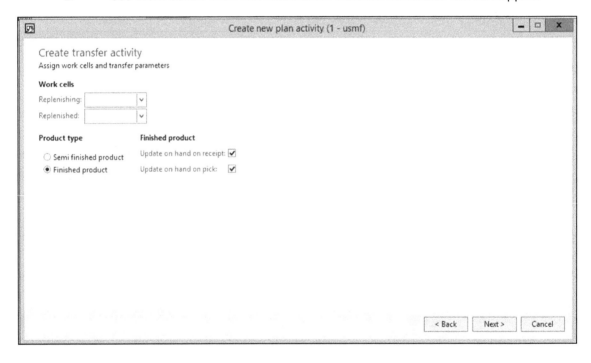

7. In the Warehouse from field, enter or select a value.

8. In the Location from field, enter or select a value.

9. In the Warehouse to field, enter or select a value.

10. In the Location to field, enter or select a value.

11. Click Next.

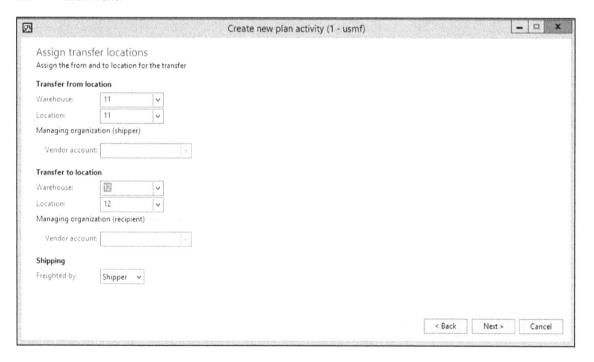

12.   In the Time(s) field, enter a number.

13.   Click Next.

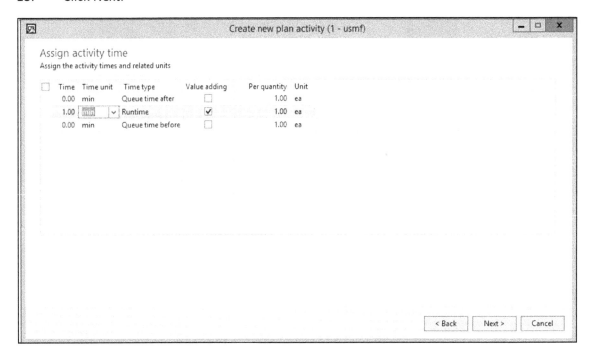

14.   Click Finish.

15.   Click Close and Activate Production Flow Version.

Production Flows - Chained

Note: Instructions precede screen copies

Typically used with Sales Event kanbans

See Production Flow Version for production flow version creation

1.	Click Create new plan activity in the <u>upstream</u> production flow.

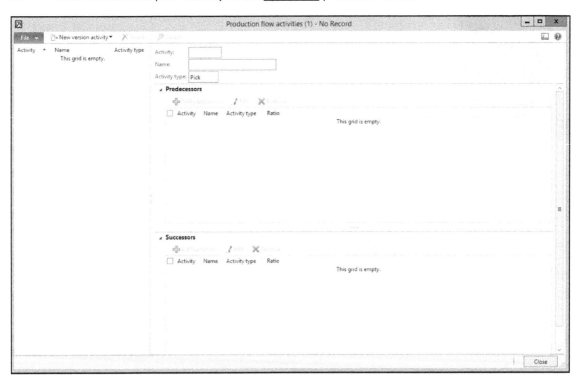

2.   Click Next.

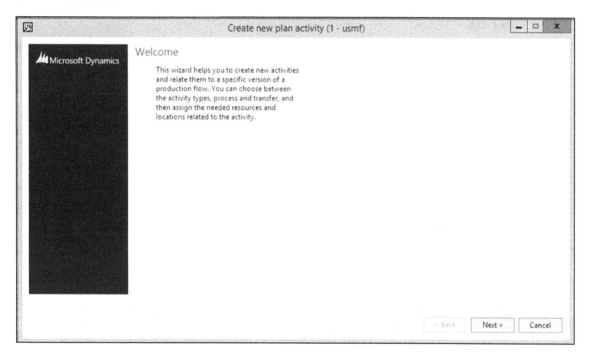

3.   In the Name field, type a value.

4.   Select Yes in the Feeds to downstream flow field.

5.   Click Next.

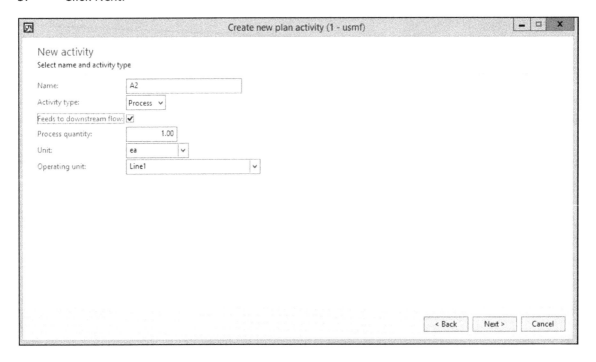

6.   In the Work cell field, enter or select a value.

7.   Click Next.

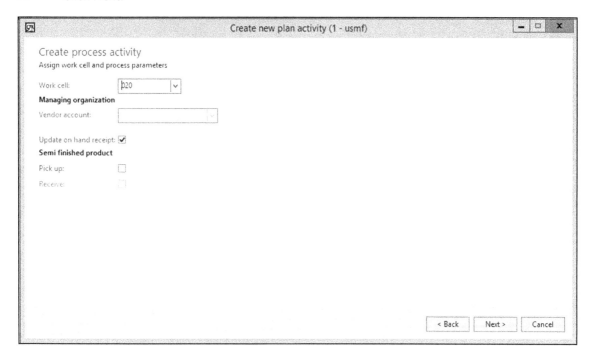

8.   Click Next.

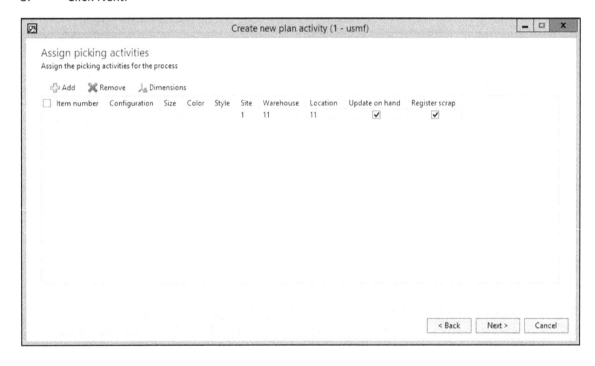

9.   Update Time(s).

10.   Click Next.

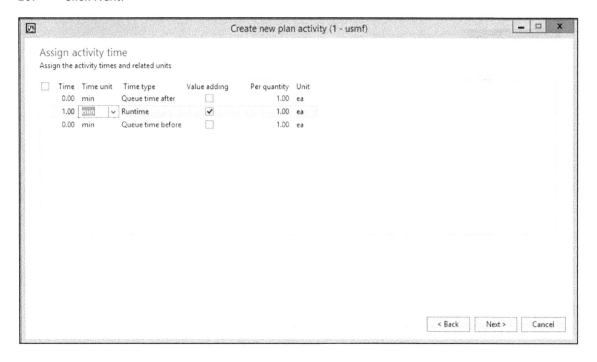

11.   Click Finish.

12. Close the page.

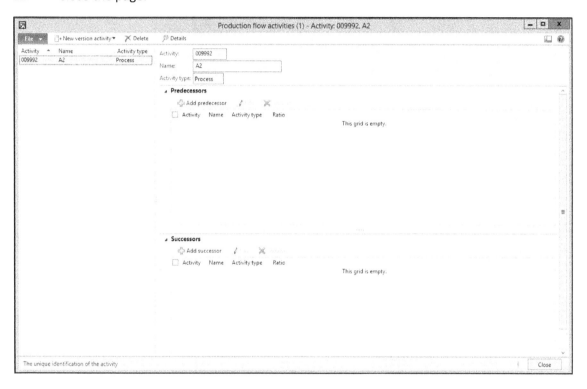

13. Click Create new plan activity in the <u>downstream</u> production flow.

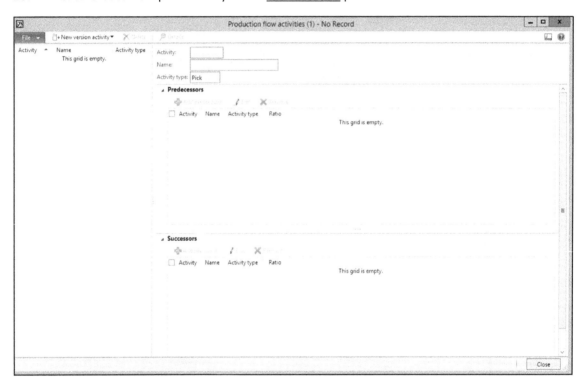

14.   Click Next.

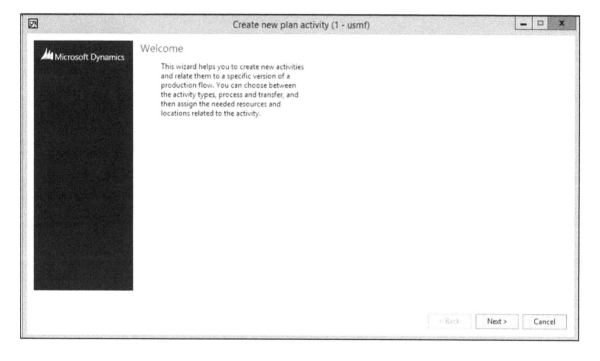

Create new plan activity (1 - usmf)

Microsoft Dynamics

Welcome

This wizard helps you to create new activities
and relate them to a specific version of a
production flow. You can choose between
the activity types, process and transfer, and
then assign the needed resources and
locations related to the activity.

< Back   Next >   Cancel

15.   In the Name field, type a value.

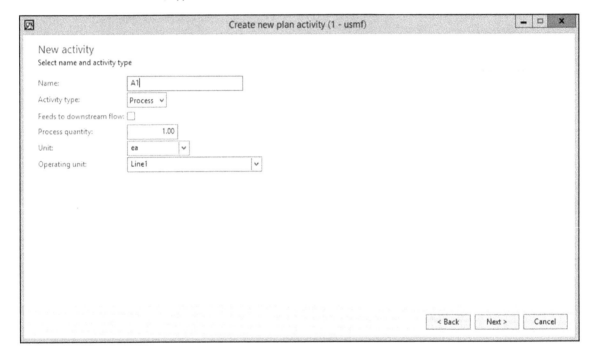

16.   In the Work cell field, enter or select a value.

17.   Click Next.

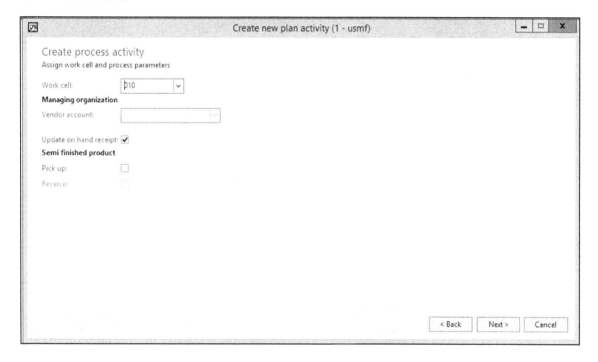

18.   Click Next.

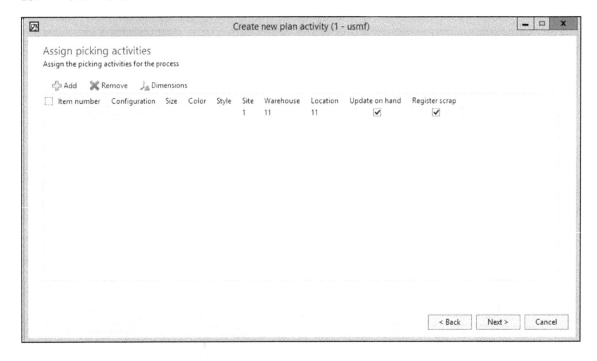

19.   Update Time(s).

20.   Click Next.

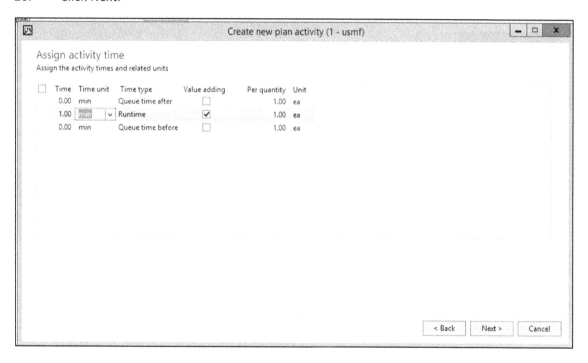

21.   Click Finish.

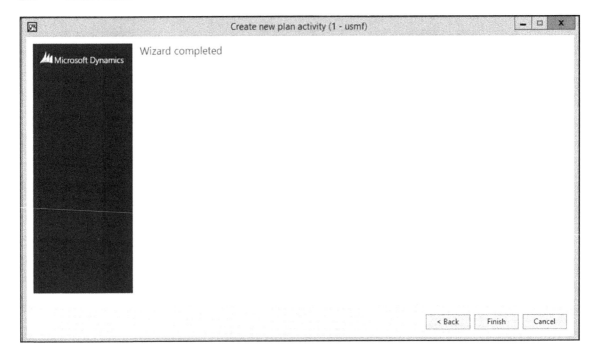

22.   Click Add predecessor.

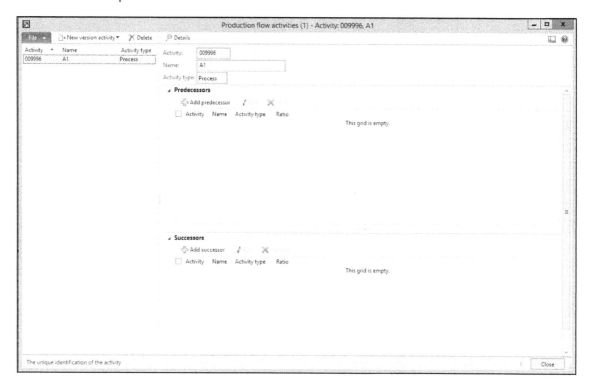

23.   Click in the Activity field.

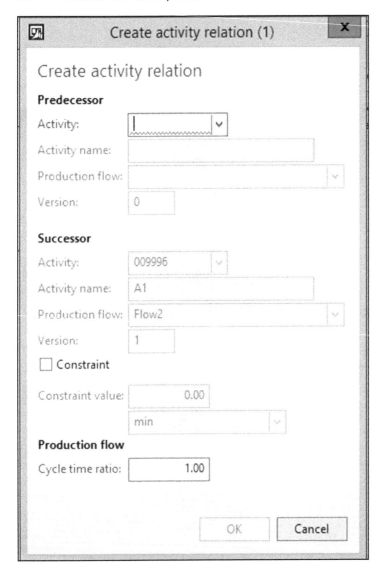

Create activity relation (1)

Create activity relation

Predecessor

Activity:

Activity name:

Production flow:

Version: 0

Successor

Activity: 009996

Activity name: A1

Production flow: Flow2

Version: 1

☐ Constraint

Constraint value: 0.00

min

Production flow

Cycle time ratio: 1.00

OK   Cancel

24. **In the Switch view field, select 'Feeder'.**

25. In the list, select the <u>upstream</u> production flow activity. (Note, this activity is listed because the 'feeds to downstream flow' flag was enabled)

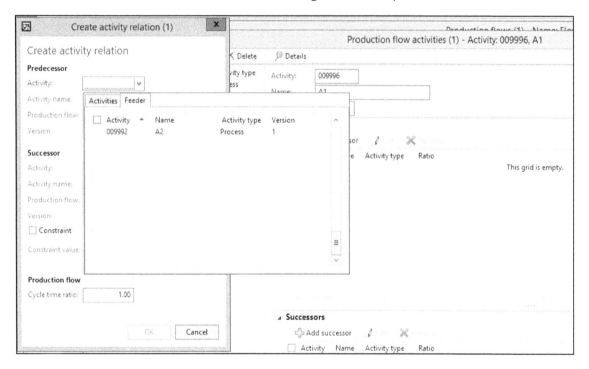

26. In the Cycle time ratio field, enter a number. (if applicable)

27. Click OK.

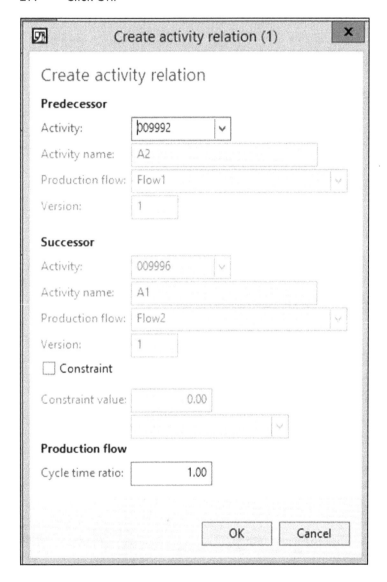

28.   Click Save.

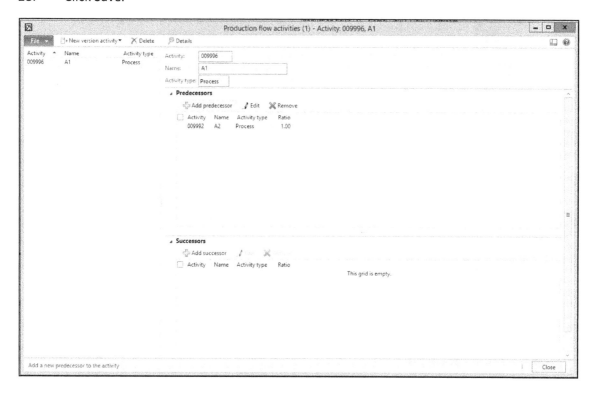

29.   Note, both production flows will need to be activated.

Kanban Rules - Fixed Non Circulating

Note: Instructions precede screen copies

1. Click 'Kanban Rule' button.

2. Example uses Type, Manufacturing, single activity

3. **Replenishment strategy defaults to Fixed**.

4. In the First plan activity field, select a value.

   1. Note, if using a multiple activity production flow, turn on the multiple activities flag and select the ending activity for multiple activity production flows. A Production Flow path is also defined via this setup step.

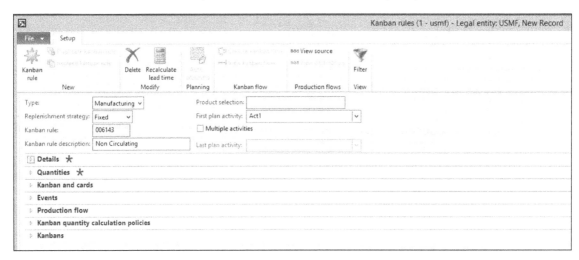

5.   In the Product field, select a value.

1.   Product families are not enabled for fixed.

6.   In the Default quantity field, enter a number.

7.   In the Fixed kanban quantity field, enter a number.

8.   In the Automatic planning quantity field, enter 1.

1.   Auto planning flag = 0, kanban is NOT planned.

2.   Auto planning flag = 1, kanban is created Planned.

3.   Auto planning flag >=2, quantity of kanbans accumulated prior to creating the kanbans as Planned.

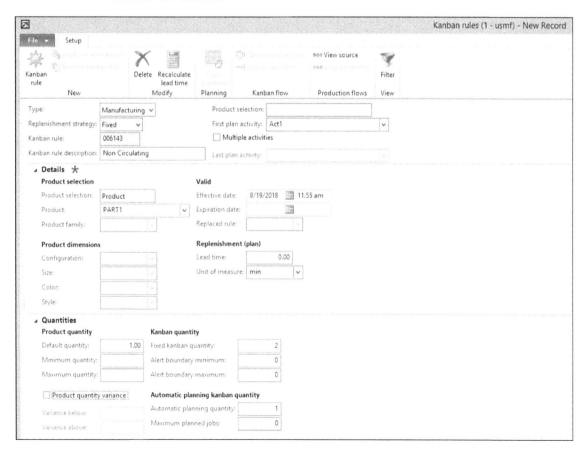

9.   On the Kanbans fast tab, click Add.

10.   If Add button is greyed out save via Ctrl S

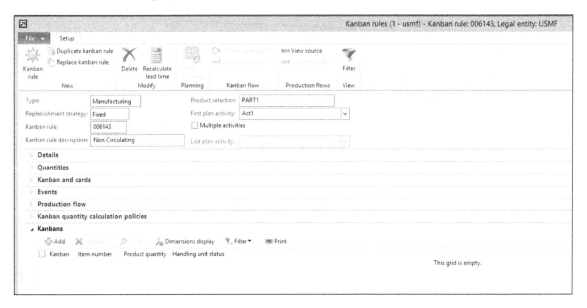

11. Enter number of kanbans.

12. Click Create. (note, print button is enabled)

13. Note, quantity calculation are not covered in this document.

14. If print check box was enabled physical card will also appear.

15. Infolog on card create status is also provided.

16. In this example 2 cards were planned because the Auto Planning flag was set. Otherwise cards would have been created unplanned. (see above)

17. Click Close.

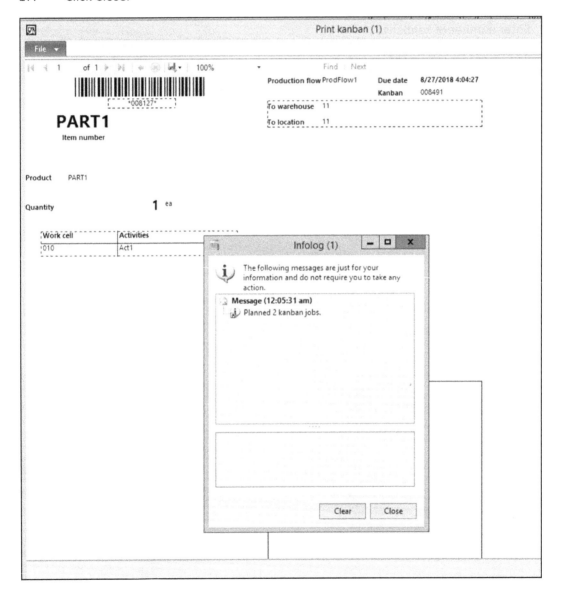

18.   Note number of non-circulating kanbans created. (to see job status, and/or cancel kanbans, click Details)

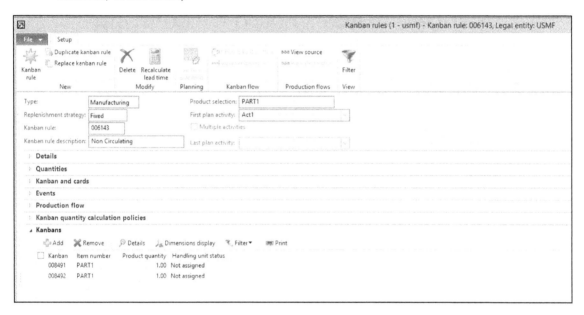

Kanban Rules - Fixed Circulating

Note: Instructions precede screen copies

1.   Click Kanban Rule.

2.   Replenishment strategy defaults to Fixed.

3.   In the First plan activity field, select a value.

   1.   Note, if using a multiple activity production flow, turn on the multiple activities
   flag and select the ending activity for multiple activity production flows. A
   Production Flow path is also defined via this setup step.

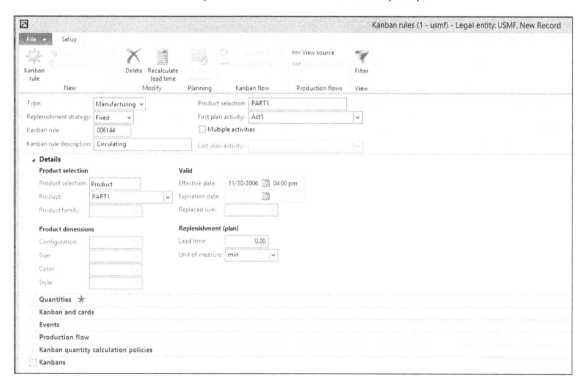

4. In the Product field, select a value.

    1. Product families are not enabled for fixed.

5. In the Default quantity field, enter a number.

6. In the Fixed kanban quantity field, enter a number.

7. In the Automatic planning quantity field, enter 1.

    1. Auto planning flag = 0, kanban is NOT planned.

    2. Auto planning flag = 1, kanban is created Planned.

    3. Auto planning flag >=2, quantity of kanbans accumulated prior to creating the
        kanbans as Planned.

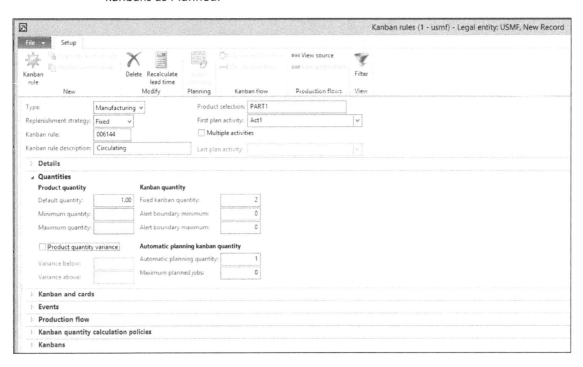

8.   From the Kanban and Cards fast tab, **select the Circulating cards check box**.

9.   In the Card assignment field, select an option. Automatic is the default.

10. Click Create cards.

11. Enter number of new cards.

    1.   Will default to the quantity entry applied above.

12. Click Create.

    1.   Cards will still need to be added to the Kanban fast tab (see below)

    2.   Turn off Print if applicable

    3.   Click view cards to see circulating card creation

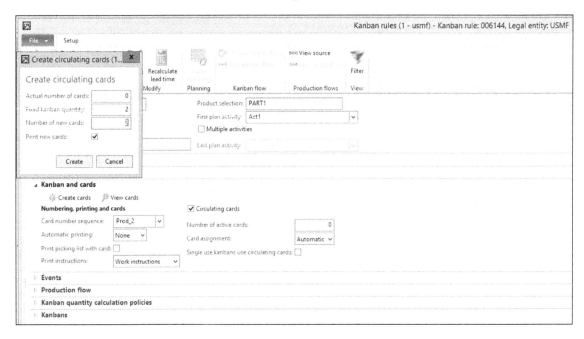

13. Close the page.

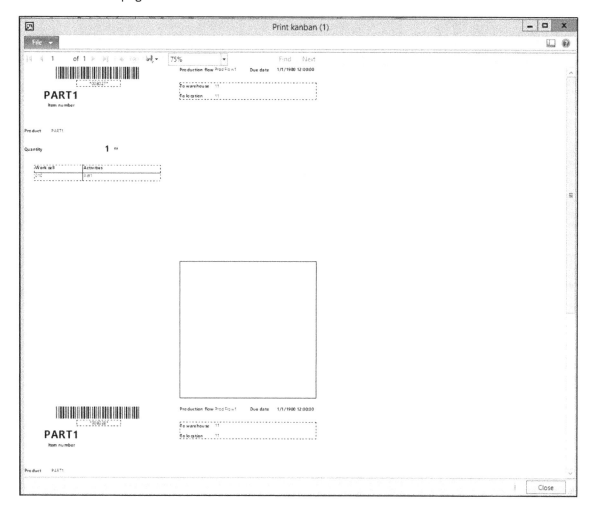

14.   From Kanbans fast tab click Add.

15.   If Add is greyed out save via Ctrl S

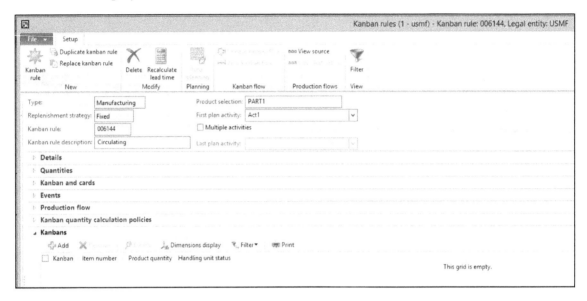

16.   Click number of new kanbans.

17.   Click Create.

18. Note created cards. Kanban #'s are the same as those that can be seen in View Cards on the Kanban and Cards fast tab. #'s will be re-used when cards are emptied. (to see job status, and/or cancel kanbans, click Details)

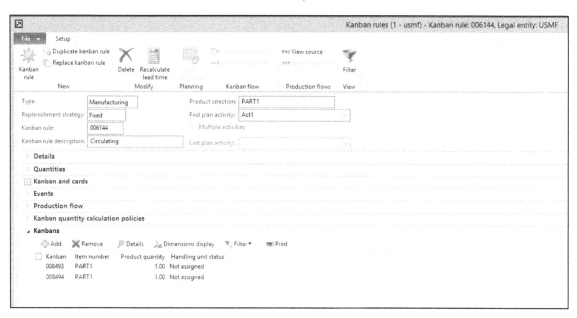

Kanban Rules - Scheduled

Note: Instructions precede screen copies

1. Click Kanban Rule.

2. **In the Replenishment strategy field, select Scheduled**. (discrete setup is not covered in this document)

    1. Scheduled kanbans are converted to kanbans in the planned orders screen via firming. Planned order type kanbans are created by Master Planning using the relevant coverage setting applicable to the part.

    2. Planned order type kanbans can be automatically firmed via coverage settings, and will create the kanban as either unplanned or planned via the automatic planning quantity that is defined on the kanban rule.

3.   In the First plan activity field, enter or select a value.

    1.   Note, if using a multiple activity production flow, turn on the multiple activities flag and select the ending activity for multiple activity production flows. A Production Flow path is also defined via this setup step.

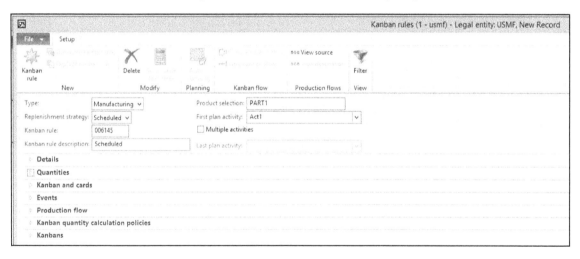

4.   In the Product field, type or select a value.

    1.   Product families are enabled by using Item Allocation Keys via a selection of Families in the Product Selection field. IAK's are used as Kanban families by Kanban Rules.

5.   In the Default quantity field, enter a number.

6.   In the Automatic planning quantity field, enter a number.

    1.   Auto planning flag = 0, kanban is NOT planned.

    2.   Auto planning flag = 1, kanban is created Planned.

    3.   Auto planning flag >=2, quantity of kanbans accumulated prior to creating the kanbans as Planned.

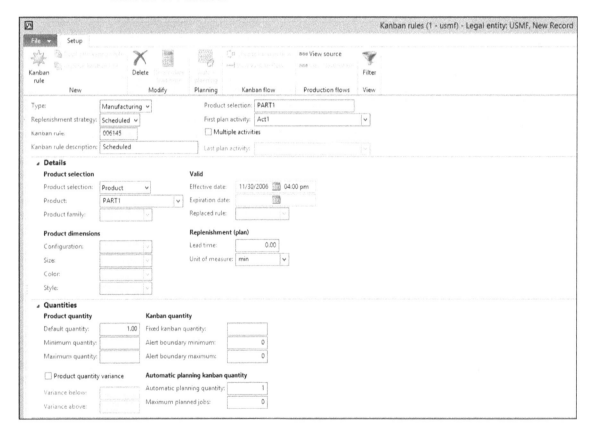

7.   Click Save.

Kanban Rules - Event, all

Note: Instructions precede screen copies

1.   Click Kanban Rule.

2.   **In the Replenishment strategy field, select Event.**

3.   In the First plan activity field, enter or select a value.

   1.   Note, if using a multiple activity production flow, turn on the multiple activities flag and select the ending activity for multiple activity production flows. A Production Flow path is also defined via this setup step.

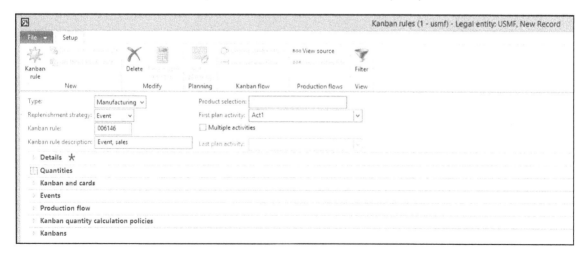

4.   In the Product field, select a value.

   1.   Product families are enabled by using Item Allocation Keys via an assignment of family in the Product Selection field.

5.   In the Automatic planning quantity field, enter a number. (note, quantity is greyed out)

   1.   Auto planning flag = 0, kanban is NOT planned.

   2.   Auto planning flag = 1, kanban is created Planned.

   3.   Auto planning flag >=2, quantity of kanbans accumulated prior to creating the kanbans as Planned.

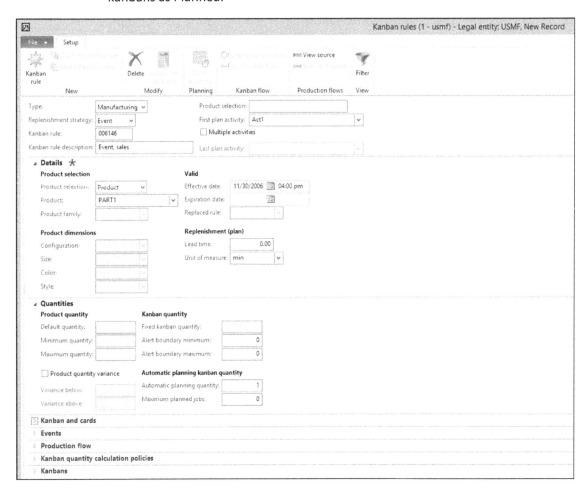

6.   In the Sales event field, select an option and set to automatic.

7.   Other Event options:

1.   BOM Line event: Generate kanban from a discrete production bill of material (discrete is not covered in this document)

2.   Kanban Line event: Generate kanban from a kanban (Note, requires chained production flows)

3.   Stock Replenishment event: Generate kanban from item coverage min (Note, not max)

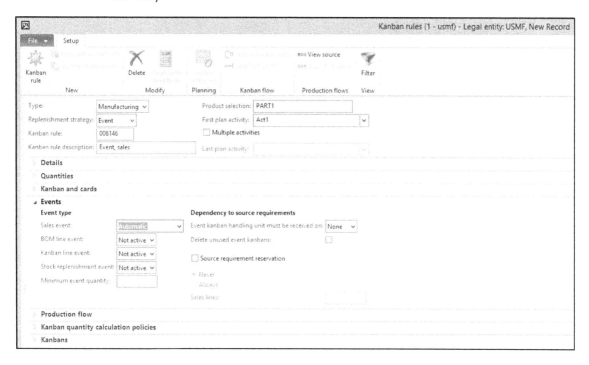

8.   Click Close.

9.   If any of the above are set to batch, set Pegging event processing under Periodic > Lean Manufacturing.

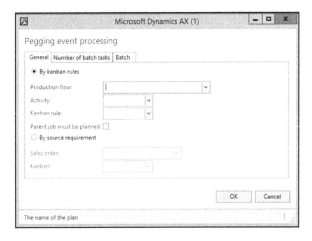

Kanban Rules - Withdrawal

Note: Instructions precede screen copies

1.   Click Kanban Rule.

2.   **In the Type field, select Withdrawal**. (defined as Transfer on Production Flow)

3.   In the First plan activity field, enter or select a value.

      1.   Note, only transfer activities are listed.

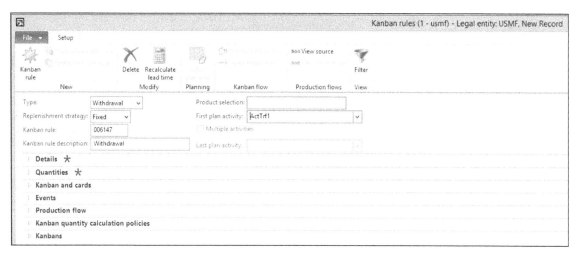

4. In the Product field, select a value.

5. In the Default quantity field, enter quantities. (Note, example is fixed kanban)

   1. Note auto planned flag is greyed out. All transfer orders start unplanned.

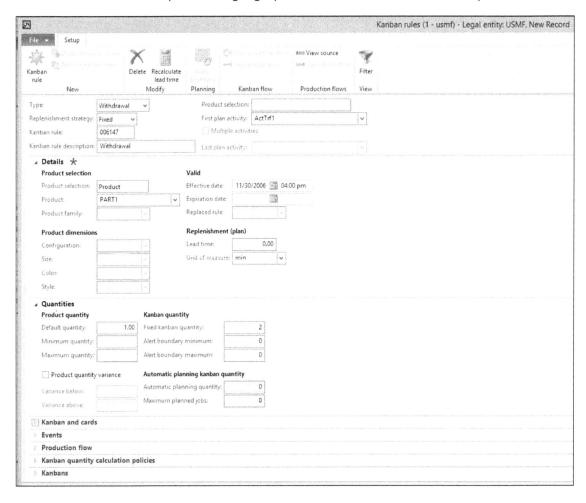

6.   Click Add. (Note, example is fixed kanban)

7.   Click Create.

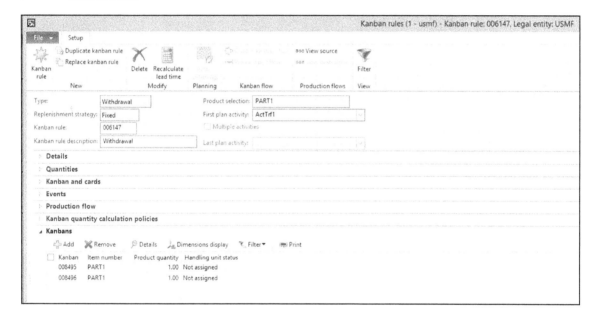

8.   Click Save.

Kanban Schedule Board

Note: Instructions precede screen copies

Examples: Planned kanban schedule change. Planning an unplanned kanban.

1.   Go to Production control > Lean Mfg > Kanban schedule board.

2.   Select work cell if applicable.

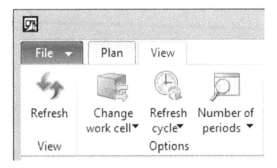

3. Planned cards appear on the grid

4. Unplanned cards are listed below on the Unplanned tab

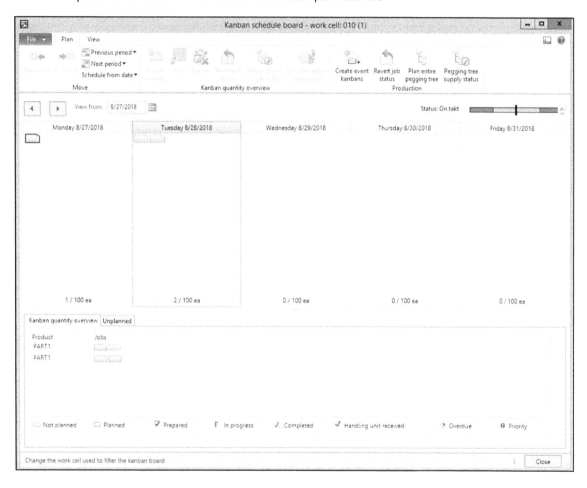

5.   Select a card on the board, and drag and drop in to another day

6.   Kanban is replanned manually for the selected time period, in this example Monday to Wednesday

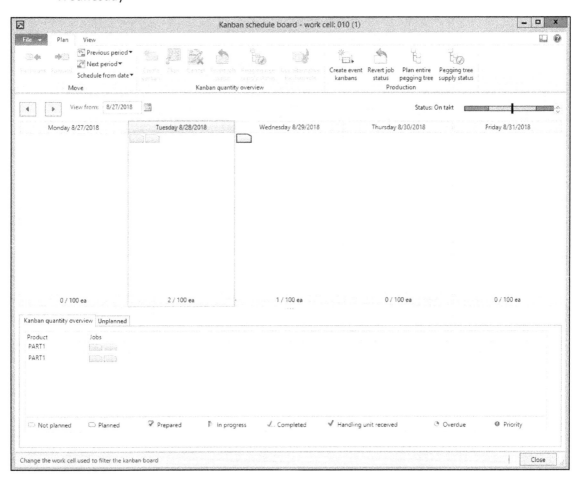

7. To plan an unplanned kanban click the unplanned at the bottom of the form.

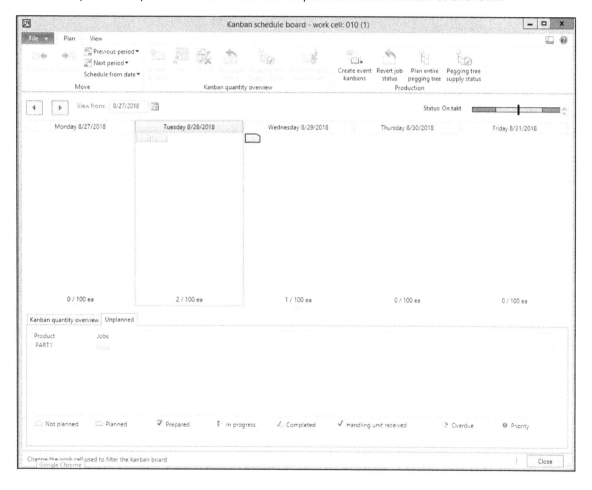

8.   Drag and drop the unplanned kanban in to the desired period.

9.   The unplanned card is now planned, in this example to Thursday.

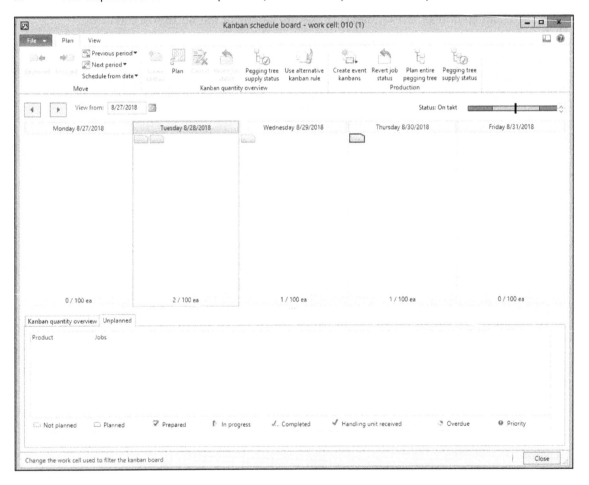

Notes:

Planned kanbas appear on the kanban board for process jobs, unplanned kanbans do not.

Click on card icon to open the card.

Kanban Board for Process Jobs

Note: Instructions precede screen copies

1.   Go to Production control > Lean Manufacturing > Kanban board for process jobs.

2.   Select the work cell if required. (Change cell button at right of form)

3.   In the list, find and select the desired record.

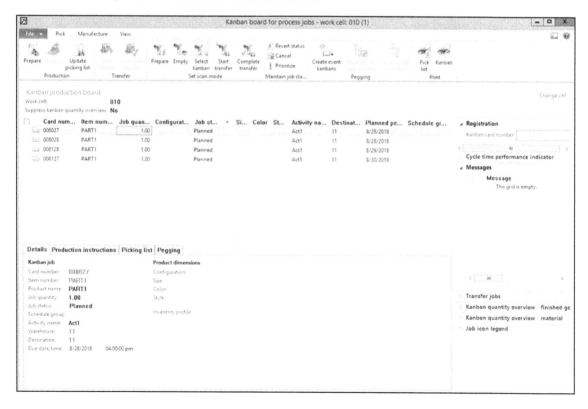

4.   Click Prepare (from action tab at top), note job status.

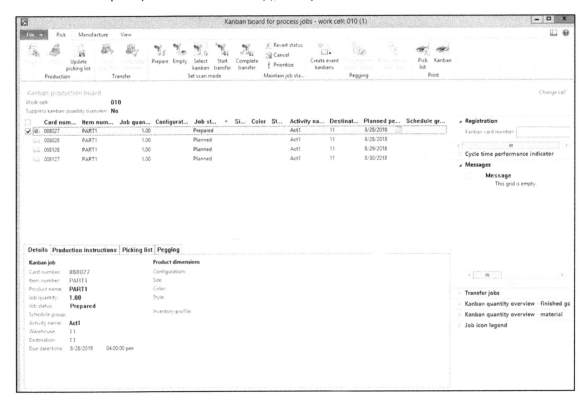

5. From the Manufacture action tab click Start (note <u>not</u> in set scan mode sub section), note job status is now 'In progress'.

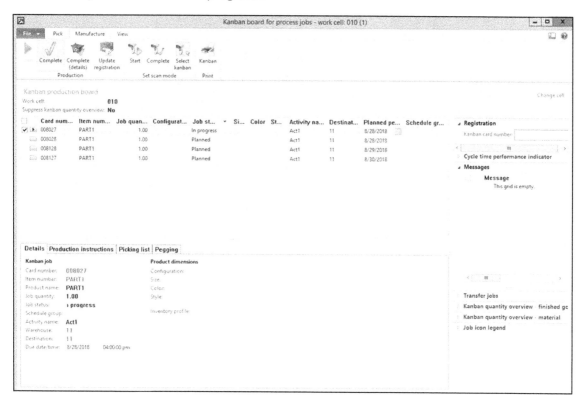

6. Click Complete (note <u>not</u> in set scan mode sub section)

7. Enter quantity updates if required.

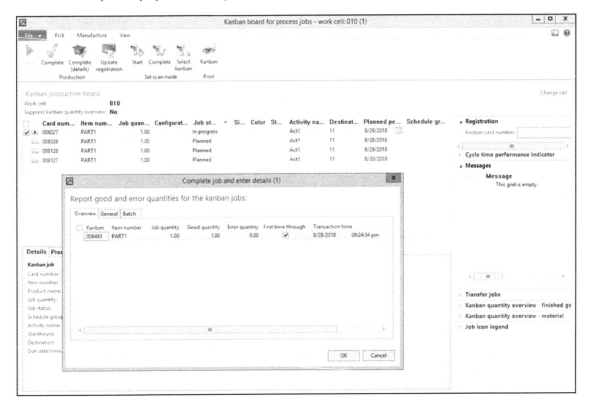

8. Notes

    1. Click on card number to open card.

    2. Revert status, cancel, prioritize, can be found on action tab.

    3. If applicable error messages appear on 'Messages' at right.

9. Product is incremented in to inventory. (part is set to Site Whse)

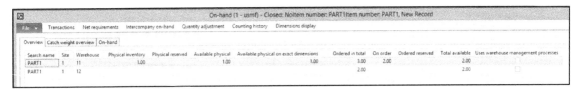

Kanban Board for Transfer Jobs

Note: Instructions precede screen copies

1.   Go to Production control > Lean Manufacturing > Kanban board for transfer jobs.

2.   Update the Filters section if required using filter button at right.

3.   Filter pop up appears, select relevant parameters.

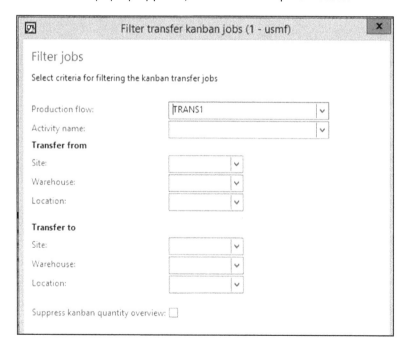

4. Select row and click Start. (not Start in the set registration mode section)

5. Note status changed from not planned to In progress)

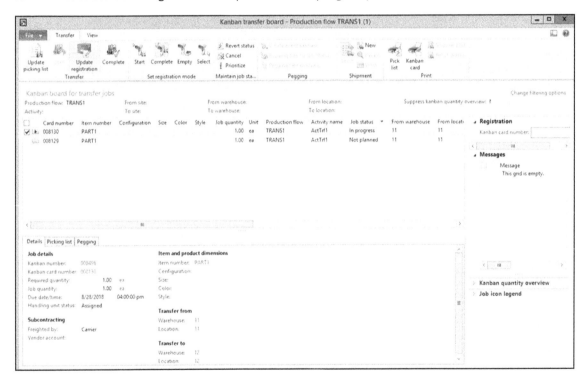

6. Click Complete. (note status)

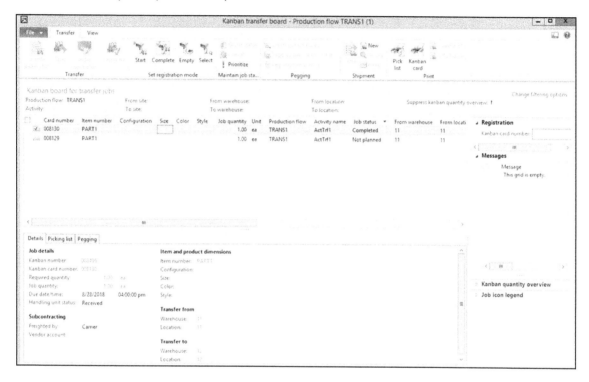

7. Product is transferred.

END

NOTES

www.ingramcontent.com/pod-product-compliance
Lightning Source LLC
Chambersburg PA
CBHW060156060326
40690CB00018B/4128